ALLAN FREWIN JONES

Unquiet Graves

Retold by Margaret Tarner

MACMILLAN

ELEMENTARY LEVEL

Founding Editor: John Milne

The Macmillan Readers provide a choice of enjoyable reading materials for learners of English. The series is published at six levels – Starter, Beginner, Elementary, Pre-intermediate, Intermediate and Upper.

Level control

Information, structure and vocabulary are controlled to suit the students' ability at each level.

The number of words at each level:

Starter	about 300 basic words
Beginner	about 600 basic words
Elementary	about 1100 basic words
Pre-intermediate	about 1400 basic words
Intermediate	about 1600 basic words
Upper	about 2200 basic words

Vocabulary

Some difficult words and phrases in this book are important for understanding the story. Some of these words are explained in the story and some are shown in the pictures. From Pre-intermediate level upwards, words are marked with a number like this: ...³. These words are explained in the Glossary at the end of the book.

Contents

A Note About This Story

The four friends in this story go to the same school. They are all members of their school's archeology club. Archeology is the study of how people lived many years ago. Archeologists dig in the ground. They try to find the things which people used and the places where they lived.

The four friends are on holiday from their school. In Britain, most schools divide their year into three terms. These terms are separated by long holidays – at Christmas, at Easter, and in the middle of the summer. But there is also a short holiday half way through each term. This is called a half-term holiday.

In this story, the friends are helping at an archeological site – a 'dig'. At these sites, archeologists dig in the ground. They try to find things which tell them about the lives of people in the past. The dig in the story is at the remains of an old village. All the people who lived in the village – the inhabitants – had to leave it at the end of the eighteenth century. After the inhabitants had left, the village remained empty – it was a 'deserted' village.

This story takes place in Norfolk – a county in the eastern part of England.

Allan Frewin Jones has written many other stories about the four friends in this book. Some of them are: *The Wicker Man*, *The Plague Pit*, *The Phantom Airman*, *The Wreckers* and *The Monk's Curse*. These books are translated into many languages.

The People in This Story

Frankie Fitzgerald

Regan Vanderlinden

Jack Christmas

Tom Christmas

Leo Gardener

Mrs Tinker

Edward Musgrave

1

The Graveyard

Three friends – a boy and two girls – were standing near an old church in Norfolk. One of the girls was Frankie Fitzgerald. She was thirteen years old and she had fair hair. The other girl had long dark hair, very pale skin and bright blue eyes. She was Regan Vanderlinden and she was eleven. The boy's name was Tom Christmas and his hair was fair. He was twelve years old. Frankie and Tom were British, but Regan was an American.

The three friends were cold. It was early afternoon, but the air was full of damp, white mist. It was difficult to see anything through the mist.

'What a terrible place!' Tom Christmas said. 'Why didn't we stay at home? Why are we spending our half-term holiday here? Do we really want to dig up an old village? *Why* did we listen to Mrs Tinker? I don't like old churches and their graveyards in this weather!'

The dark-haired girl laughed.

'Are you frightened of ghosts, Tom?' she asked. 'Do all these dead people in their graves scare you?'

'*You* scare me more than the dead people, Regan,' Tom replied. 'With your face, you could be in a horror movie!'

'This place could be in a horror movie,' Frankie said.

At that moment, the friends heard the long grass moving. Then two people – a boy and a man – came through the mist towards them.

'Did you find the keys, Jack?' Frankie called.

'Yes, they were in Leo's car,' the boy answered.

Jack Christmas was Tom's brother. He was a year older

than Tom and he had fair hair and thoughtful brown eyes. The young man with Jack was Leo Gardener. Leo was an archeologist and he was a friend of the kids' history teacher, Mrs Tinker. Leo was tall and thin. He had long hair and a beard.

The kids were a long way from their homes, but Leo lived in the nearby town. He took care of an archeological site near the church.

The four friends were all very interested in history and archeology. They were members of their school's archeology club. They had come to Norfolk for a few days with Mrs Tinker. They wanted to learn more about archeology.

Leo's archeological site was an old ruined village. All the walls of the houses were broken down, and only the church was still complete. No one had lived in the village for more than two hundred years – it was deserted. Because no one lived in the village, the church was not used any longer. But Leo had the keys of the building and now the kids were going to look inside it.

The church with its tall tower stood in the middle of a large graveyard. Many people had been buried there when the village was inhabited. Around the graveyard was a thick, dark hedge. Leo pushed open the gate in the hedge and he led Frankie, Regan, Tom and Jack into the graveyard.

The four friends looked around at the gravestones. The stones were very old and some of them had fallen over. There were names and other words carved on the gravestones, but they were very difficult to read.

'Well, here's the church,' Leo said. He stopped in front of the old grey building. 'Parts of it are nearly nine hundred years old.'

The four friends looked around at the gravestones.

Leo walked up to the church door and unlocked it with a big key. At that moment, his mobile phone started to ring.

'You all go inside,' the young man said to the four friends. 'I'll join you in a minute.'

Jack pushed open the heavy door and the four friends went slowly inside the church.

The air in the old building was very cold. Light came into the church from a beautiful window in the tower. The kids moved very quietly.

Regan walked up to a square of stone with words carved on it – a plaque. It was fixed to one of the walls. Tom walked up behind her and he read the words in a quiet voice.

'To the memory of Hugo Glanville, improving squire of Isenglas. He was murdered by a villain in the year 1778. Let him rest in peace.'

'What does it mean?' Regan asked. 'What is an "improving squire"? You British people use some strange phrases!'

'The squire owned all the land round here,' Tom told her. 'He lived in a big house – Isenglas Hall. I don't know what he improved. Maybe he improved the village. Maybe he improved the lives of the villagers. Maybe he built better houses for the poor people.'

Suddenly, the four friends heard Leo calling them. A moment later, the young man hurried into the church.

'I'm sorry, kids,' he said quickly. 'I've got to leave you. And I need to lock the church, so you'll have to go outside now.'

'Leave the keys with us, Leo,' Frankie said. 'Then we can stay here longer.'

'OK,' Leo said. 'Here they are. Don't forget to lock the door when you leave. Then go straight back to the camp. Stay together and don't get lost!'

Leo hurried away. The kids walked slowly around the old church. They saw many more plaques. Many people were buried inside the church.

'This a strange place,' Frankie said. 'It's full of dead people.'

'Yes,' Jack said quietly. 'I can feel something strange too. Something or someone is watching us. Watching and waiting —'

The other three friends looked at Jack. He often knew things which he couldn't explain. Sometimes he knew what was going to happen *before* it happened. He often had strange feelings and he often said strange things. And when he said these things, he was usually right.

'Let's get out of here,' Regan said. 'I've seen enough.'

The others agreed with her. Soon the four of them were standing in the graveyard again. Frankie locked the church door carefully, then she put the keys in her pocket.

2

The Horror in the Vault

Outside the church, the mist was a little thinner. The thick hedge round the graveyard looked very dark. The kids could see the gravestones more clearly now. They could see another building in the graveyard too.

'What's that?' Regan asked the others. 'Let's have a look.'

The friends walked across the graveyard to a little stone building. The old building was square, with a flat roof and no windows. There were two black iron gates in front of its dark wooden doors. And there was a picture carved in the stone above the doors.

'This is very strange,' Jack said, looking at the picture. 'It's a carving of a wolf with a small boy. Look, the animal's foot is on the child's shoulder. Is the wolf guarding the child? Or is it going to kill him?'

The kids looked at the strange picture. The name 'Glanville' was carved in the stone beneath it.

'Glanville,' said Regan. 'That was the "improving squire's" name. What's this place for, Jack?'

'It's a family vault,' Jack replied. 'All the dead Glanvilles are lying inside, in big wooden coffins.'

'Are they buried under the ground?' Regan asked.

'No, vaults are the rooms under the ground,' Jack told her. 'There are steps inside this building which go down into the vault. The coffins are usually put on shelves around the walls. Do you want to see them?'

'No, thank you!' Regan answered quickly. 'And we can't get inside because the gates are locked.'

'You're afraid!' Tom said with a smile. 'You're scared of all those dead bodies!'

'I'm not scared of anything!' Regan shouted. 'I'm not even scared of you!' She ran towards Tom and he began to run towards the back of the building.

A few moments later there was a loud noise. Then there was a shout from Tom.

'Help! Help me!' he shouted.

Frankie and Jack laughed.

'Regan has caught him!' Jack said. 'Bad luck for Tom!'

Then Regan came running back towards them. She was laughing too.

'Tom's in a hole. Come and help him,' she said.

Frankie and Jack followed Regan to the other side of the vault. Tom was sitting on the grass, near the wall. His left leg was buried deep in the ground.

'Help me!' he said. 'Regan pushed me and my leg went down a hole. I can't get it out.'

Frankie and Jack held Tom's shoulders and they pulled hard. Tom's leg came out of the hole suddenly and they all fell on the ground.

'You're a fool, Tom,' Frankie said. Then she gave a cry. The ground had opened up in front of her. Frankie began to slide down into a big black hole. Jack tried to stop her. He held her arm. But the hole was getting bigger each moment. Suddenly there was a roaring noise and Jack slid down into the hole after Frankie.

Tom and Regan stared in horror at the black hole.

Inside the vault, Frankie was lying on the cold, damp floor. Her knee and ankle hurt. There was a bad smell in the vault and it was very dark. A moment later, she heard a noise nearby.

'Jack, is that you?' Frankie asked. 'Are you OK?'

'Yes — Yes, I'm OK,' Jack said. 'But my leg hurts. We've fallen about three metres. Can you see anything?'

'No, but I can feel something,' Frankie said. 'I can feel one of the coffins. Jack, this place is full of dead people! It's full of rotting people and old bones. And the coffins are all rotting too. You can smell them. This is a horrible place!'

'You're right. We must get out of here,' Jack said.

'Don't worry, the others will help us.'

Jack shouted up to the others, 'Hey! Tom! Regan!'

'What are you doing down there?' Regan shouted back. 'Shall we go for help, or can you get out?'

'We'll try to get out,' Jack replied. 'There are shelves round the walls. We can climb up onto them. Then you can pull us out.'

He turned to look at Frankie.

'It's OK,' Jack told her. 'We can get out. Come on, I'll help you. You can go first.'

'I can't,' Frankie said. 'I can't move. I'm too frightened to move. There are coffins on those shelves. They have dead bodies inside. I can't touch them! There's something horrible here. If I touch a coffin, something dead will pull me inside!'

'No, it won't, Frankie,' Jack said kindly. 'Listen, I'll help you. Come on, Frankie – please!'

Jack held the girl's hands and helped her to stand. Frankie was shaking with fear. Jack pushed her hands onto a cold stone shelf. Frankie tried to pull them away. Then she felt something under her hand. It was small and made of metal. She picked it up. Suddenly, she felt a strange power moving through her body.

Jack felt the power too. It was as strong as an electric shock! Frankie gave a little scream. Then she smiled in the darkness.

'It's OK, Jack,' she said. 'The dead people can't hurt me now. I know that. I can climb out now. Let's go, please.'

Half a minute later, Jack and Frankie were standing beside their friends.

'Was the vault full of coffins?' Tom asked his brother.

'Yes,' Jack replied. 'It was horrible. I don't want to go back there.'

Frankie said nothing. She was looking down at her open hand.

'What have you got there?' Regan asked her friend.

'It's half of a coin,' Frankie said. 'It's very old. There's something strange about it too.'

'Let me see,' Jack said. He held out his hand.

'No!' Frankie said quickly. 'Don't touch it. I found it. It's mine!'

Jack was surprised, but he said nothing.

'Show it to Mrs Tinker,' Regan said. 'Maybe it's made of silver. Maybe it's worth a lot of money.'

'Mrs Tinker's *not* going to have it. It's mine. *I'm* going to keep it!' Frankie said. She spoke in a hard, angry voice. 'Let's get back to the camp now. I'm hungry.'

Frankie began to walk quickly away. The others followed her silently.

Outside the graveyard, the mist had disappeared and the sun was shining.

'What a lovely day!' Frankie said. 'I feel happy again. Look! Mrs Tinker's car is coming down the road. She'll drive us to the campsite.'

An old car stopped by the side of the road and the children quickly got into it.

'Did you like the church?' Mrs Tinker asked them. Then she saw their clothes. 'Jack, your clothes are dirty! And so are yours, Frankie. What have you been doing?'

'Frankie fell into an old vault,' Regan said. 'Then Jack fell in too. Frankie found part of a coin down there. Show it to Mrs Tinker, Frankie.'

'No,' Frankie said quickly. 'I can't. I've lost it.'

'That's not true. It's in your pocket,' Regan said.

The older girl gave her friend a strange, angry look. For a moment, Frankie's face seemed old and evil. Then she pulled the half-coin from her pocket and gave it to her teacher.

Mrs Tinker looked at the half-coin carefully.

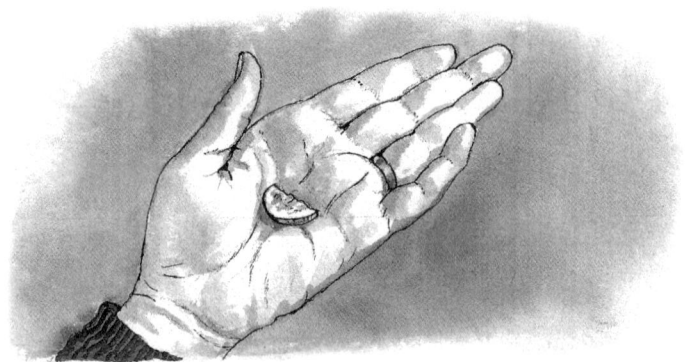

'It's very old,' the teacher said. 'Someone cut the coin in half years many ago.'

'Why did they do that?' Regan asked.

'I don't know,' Mrs Tinker said. 'Maybe the coin was worth a lot. Maybe someone didn't want to spend all their money. Maybe they kept the other half to spend another time.'

'Sometimes, lovers cut a coin in half,' Frankie said slowly. 'Then each of them kept one half of the coin. It helped them to remember each other when they couldn't be together.'

'Yes, you're right,' Mrs Tinker said with a smile. 'Maybe that's the true story. I'll keep the coin and I'll find out more about it for you, Frankie. But now we must get back to Leo. He's waiting for us at the campsite.'

3

The Deserted Village

Mrs Tinker soon turned her car off the road which led from the village. Now they were travelling on a small lane through Isenglas Park. To their right, the ground sloped down to a large lake. The water was bright in the sunshine. To their left, the ground sloped upwards. At the top of the little hill stood Isenglas Hall.

Nobody lived in the old house now. It had been empty for a long time and no one took care of it.

Mrs Tinker stopped her car by a gate next to the lane. Jack got out and opened the gate. Mrs Tinker drove through it, into a field. She stopped.

In front of them was the archeological site – the dig. The area was a square and each side was about a hundred metres long. The grass had been removed from the site. Leo Gardener and some other archeologists had dug down to the ruins of the deserted village. The kids could see parts of the walls of the old houses. They could see the floors of rooms and passages, and they could see parts of stairways.

Leo was taking photographs of the site. He smiled at the kids and their teacher.

'It's good to see you again,' he said. 'Your tents and sleeping bags are in my caravan. Put up your tents now. Then we'll eat. And can I have the church keys, please, Frankie?'

Mrs Tinker put up her tent very quickly. Tom and Jack worked hard and their tent was soon up too. But the two girls were having a problem.

This was the first time that Regan had put up a tent. She usually stayed in big hotels with her rich parents.

Frankie laughed.

'You're not helping, Regan,' she said. 'You're making things worse! Let me put up the tent by myself. Go and do something else for ten minutes!'

'OK,' Regan said. 'I'll help Mrs Tinker with the food.'

Mrs Tinker made a fire and she began to cook the food. Soon, the meal was ready.

Everybody was very hungry and, at first, no one had time to talk. They were too busy eating. But later, the kids told Leo about the hole in the ground by the Glanville vault.

'Don't worry about the hole,' Leo said. 'It wasn't your fault. No one looks after that vault now. I'll cover up the hole tomorrow. What did you see in the church? Did you see the plaque in memory of Hugo Glanville?'

'He was the improving squire. He died in 1778. Is that right?' Regan asked.

'Yes, that's right,' Leo replied. 'Isenglas Hall was his home. Hugo Glanville was murdered there. He was "murdered by a villain", as the plaque says. The murderer once lived in this village. And Hugo destroyed the village. People were angry about that.'

'The plaque calls Hugo an "improving squire", Leo,' Regan said. 'But you are telling us a different story. He didn't improve the village – he destroyed it!'

'Why did he do that?' Tom asked.

'Hugo wanted to have a large lake,' Leo told them. 'At that time, every big country house had a lake in its park. Hugo wanted to see the lake from the Hall. But the village was between the house and the lake. So he destroyed the village and "improved" the view from the house.'

'What happened to the people in the village?' Regan asked. 'Did Hugo build new houses for them?'

'No, he didn't,' Leo replied. 'He didn't care about the people. They all had to move away. They had to find somewhere else to live. They weren't happy about that.'

'No, they weren't happy!' Frankie said in a strange voice. 'They hated Hugo Glanville. They *all* hated him.'

Jack looked at Frankie with surprise. Her voice sounded cold and hard. Suddenly her face looked cruel.

'Why didn't the villagers stop Hugo's plans?' Regan asked. 'Why didn't they fight him?'

'Hugo owned all the land near the Hall,' Leo said. 'The village belonged to him. The villagers didn't own their houses – Hugo owned them. The villagers were his tenants and he was their squire.'

'So the villain who killed him was one of the villagers,' Regan said.

'He *wasn't* a villain,' Frankie said quietly.

'Maybe he wasn't,' Leo said. 'Listen, I've got a good idea. We'll take a walk in the park. You can look at the lake. And I'll tell you the story of Eleanor's Bridge.'

'Who was Eleanor?' Regan asked.

'I'll tell you when we get to the bridge!' Leo replied.

4

The Story of Eleanor's Bridge

It was a beautiful autumn evening. The sun was setting now, and the sky was red and gold. Leo walked down towards the lake and the kids followed him. The water of the lake was very still.

At one end of the lake, Leo stopped beside a little stone building. From the building, stone steps led down to the lake. Parts of the building were broken. Little trees and plants were growing all over it. There were some strange statues there too, and a stone seat.

'It looks about two thousand years old,' Regan said.

'Yes. It looks the same as some ancient buildings in Greece,' Mrs Tinker said, with a smile.

'Is it a Greek building?' Regan asked. 'How did it get here, Leo?'

'No, it's not Greek,' Leo said. 'It was built about two hundred years ago. But it was built as a ruin. Rich people loved to travel at that time. And they loved the old buildings that they saw in Greece. But most of those buildings were ruins. So rich people in this country often built their own ruins. Hugo Glanville, the improving squire, built these ruins.'

'That's horrible,' Frankie said. 'Hugo destroyed a village where people lived and he built these useless ruins. What a terrible man!'

'Lots of landowners behaved badly at that time,' Leo told her. 'They were rich, so they did what they liked. They didn't care about their tenants.'

'Yes, those were cruel times,' Mrs Tinker said.

'It looks about two thousand years old,' Regan said.

'OK, now we'll look at Eleanor's Bridge,' Leo said. The kids followed him across the grass. He took them to a bridge over a small river that flowed into the lake. The little bridge was old and broken.

Leo stopped and smiled at the kids.

'Now, do you want to hear Eleanor's story?' he asked them.

'Yes, if it's a true story,' Regan said. 'Is it true?'

'I don't know,' Leo replied. 'Nobody knows the truth. But many people believe the story.

'Eleanor was a lovely young woman,' Leo went on. 'Her parents were dead. Hugo Glanville took care of her – she was Hugo's ward. They both lived at Isenglas Hall. Eleanor was going to marry a rich neighbour. Hugo had arranged the marriage.'

'Did Eleanor *want* to marry this neighbour?' Regan asked.

'No, she did *not*,' Leo replied. 'Eleanor was only seventeen at that time and the neighbour was an old man. The marriage was Hugo's idea.'

'That was sad,' Frankie said quietly.

'But she *didn't* get married,' Leo continued. 'A few days before the wedding, a man broke into Isenglas Hall. It happened in the middle of the night. Hugo woke up and heard the man moving about. He tried to catch the man, but the man had a knife. The two of them fought and Hugo was killed. Eleanor had woken up too. She saw the fight. She saw the man kill Hugo.'

'Did somebody catch the murderer?' Tom asked.

'Yes,' Leo said. 'The man jumped out of a window, but Hugo's servants ran after him. The murderer ran into the graveyard at the church. He tried to hide in the Glanville family vault. The servants caught the man and they killed him there in the graveyard. They found a rope and they hanged him from a tree.'

'What a horrible story!' Regan said.

'But that's not the end of the story,' Leo said. 'Maybe Eleanor was unhappy because Hugo was dead. She ran out into the park and came to this little bridge. She threw herself into the water and was drowned. That's why this bridge is called Eleanor's Bridge.'

'Wait a minute!' Regan said. 'This is a very *little* river. It isn't very deep. No one could drown here.'

'Well, that's the story,' Leo said. 'But maybe you're right. Eleanor's body was never found.'

The sky was nearly dark now. The trees and bushes near the bridge were dark too. Frankie was staring at them. The shadows were black. 'Is there a black statue there too?' she asked herself. 'But why is a statue moving?'

Then Frankie saw a young man standing in the shadows. He had dark clothes and black hair. The young man stared at her. Suddenly, the girl felt very cold. The young man frightened her very much!

'Hey, Frankie!' Regan said. 'I'm talking to you!'

Frankie turned and looked at her friend. Then she looked back at the dark shadows. The young man had gone!

———

That night, Frankie could not sleep. She lay in her sleeping bag and she stared into the darkness. For a long time, she listened to Regan's quiet breathing. At last, she spoke.

'Regan?' she said quietly. But Regan was in a deep sleep.

Frankie got out of her sleeping bag. She found her torch. She walked very quietly towards Mrs Tinker's tent.

The night was cold and the dark sky was full of stars.

'Mrs Tinker,' Frankie said quietly. Her teacher did not answer. Frankie opened the tent and went inside. Yes, there was Mrs Tinker's handbag.

Frankie took the bag outside and opened it. She shone her torch into the bag. Something was shining brightly there. It was the half-coin.

A few minutes later, Frankie was in her sleeping bag again. The half-coin was in her hand. Now she could sleep!

5

In the Graveyard Again

It was eight o'clock the next morning. The kids, their teacher and Leo were at the dig early. They were ready to start work.

'We've done a lot of work here already,' Leo said. 'You can see the streets and the shapes of the houses. Your job is to clear away the remaining earth. Then we'll be able to see the shapes more clearly. OK?'

'OK,' they all said.

Everybody worked very hard all morning. At twelve o'clock, Mrs Tinker drove into the town to get some more food. Leo left the site and went to the church. He wanted to look at the Glanville family vault.

Some time later, the kids stopped working. They were ready for their lunch.

'The sun is hot now,' Regan said. 'Let's eat our lunch by the river.'

The others agreed and they all went to the river.

———

Half an hour later, all the food had been eaten. The four friends were stretched out on the grass. They felt sleepy in the hot sun. Time passed.

Suddenly, Jack sat up and gave a shout.

'Hey, Frankie! What are you doing?' he shouted.

Regan and Tom sat up too. Frankie was standing in the river! She was staring up at the old bridge. The water nearly reached her waist.

Regan ran down to the river bank.

'Frankie, come out of there!' she shouted.

Frankie smiled. 'Eleanor didn't throw herself from the bridge,' she said. 'I'm sure of that.'

Frankie walked out of the water. Her jeans were very wet.

'Is there any more food?' she asked.

'Girls!' Tom said to his brother. 'They're all mad!'

Jack laughed, and the four friends lay down on the grass again.

Half an hour later, Jack looked at his watch.

'We've been here for two hours,' he said. 'We must get back to the site and do some more work. Come on!'

'You three return to the dig. I must go to the church

first,' Frankie said. 'Leo is there, isn't he? He'll drive me back to the site.' She began to walk quickly towards the church.

'I'm going with Frankie,' Regan said quietly to the two brothers. 'I'm worried about her. What are you boys going to do?'

'We'll come too,' Jack said. 'Frankie is doing some strange things. We mustn't leave her alone.'

———

In the graveyard, Jack saw a old tree. Two of its branches stretched out towards him. Suddenly, the boy felt cold.

Somehow, the tree was bad – he knew that. Was it the tree in Leo's story? Was it the tree where Hugo Glanville's murderer had been hanged?

Leo's car was not near the church. Regan, Jack and Tom followed Frankie to the old vault in the churchyard. There were some pieces of wood across the hole in the ground. There was a large sign too.

Frankie began to move the pieces of wood.

'Hey! What are you doing?' Regan asked her.

'I'm going down there again,' Frankie said. 'I want to see Hugo's coffin.'

'Stop her!' Regan shouted to the boys. 'That place is dangerous. Frankie will get hurt!'

'Frankie, stop this! Don't be silly,' Jack said.

But Frankie's legs were already in the hole.

'I *must* see it,' she said. Her eyes looked hard and strange again. She switched on the torch which she had brought with her. In a moment, she had jumped into the vault.

6

Is Frankie Mad?

A big black bird flew overhead. It gave a loud, harsh cry.

Regan ran to the hole in the ground.

'Frankie!' she called. 'Frankie, speak to me, please!'

'Go away!' a voice replied from the hole. The voice was deep and rough. Was it Frankie's voice?

Suddenly a cold wind blew from the vault. It blew across the graveyard. Jack felt cold, very cold. And then he heard the sound of men shouting. He heard men running. There was something evil in the graveyard, something horrible. It made him think of death and murder.

The black bird cried out again. It flew across the grave-yard and landed on the church. It sat high on the church roof.

Jack was very frightened, but he looked down into the hole.

'Frankie? Are you there?' he called.

'Frankie isn't here!' a deep voice answered. 'Leave me alone. Go away!'

Jack saw a yellow light in the vault. It wasn't the light from Frankie's torch. It was the light of a candle! Jack was terribly afraid now. He looked at Regan and Tom, but they did not move or speak. What was happening to them? What was happening to Frankie?

Jack took a deep breath. He had to help Frankie quickly. He knew that!

Very carefully, he moved down into the vault. Something or someone rushed towards him.

For a moment, Jack saw a young man's face. He saw black clothes and black hair. But no – it wasn't a man. It was Frankie. Her golden hair was blowing around her head. Her face looked very, very angry.

'No! No! You won't capture me!' Frankie said.

But it was not Frankie's voice. It was a deep voice, and it was full of fear. There were shadows all around Jack. He started to fight wildly. Then he saw Frankie again. He pushed her hard. She dropped her torch and fell against the wall.

Jack picked up the torch quickly. He shone it in Frankie's face. She was in a corner of the vault and her face was hard and angry. Suddenly Jack had a new feeling – a horrible one.

'The dead people in the vault are waking up!' he thought. 'They are coming out of their coffins. They are coming for me and Frankie!'

'Don't shine that torch in my face, Jack,' Frankie said suddenly. She spoke in her usual voice. 'I wanted to see Hugo's coffin, but I couldn't find it.'

'Frankie, I must talk to you,' Jack said. 'There's something terribly wrong here.'

'Wrong? What do you mean?' the girl asked.

'Well – you were fighting me a moment ago,' Jack said.

'I'm sorry, Jack,' Frankie said. 'There were some bad people down here. I was fighting them, not you. But that's finished now. Let's get out of here.'

Frankie climbed out of the vault easily and Jack followed her. He did not understand Frankie. He did not understand anything!

'Frankie! Are you OK?' Regan asked her friend, when she was standing on the grass again.

'Yes, I'm fine,' Frankie replied. 'But I didn't find the coffin. I couldn't see very well. It's too dark and dirty down there.'

'Let's get back to the dig now,' Jack said. 'Mrs Tinker will be angry.'

'Are you really OK?' Regan asked Frankie again. 'Your voice sounded strange down there. And you've done some strange things this afternoon.'

'I don't understand you,' Frankie said. '*You* are the strange person here, not me. Don't be silly, Regan!'

Jack had been right. Mrs Tinker *was* angry when they returned to the archeological site.

'It's nearly four o'clock!' she said. 'Where were you? You came here to help. You're here to help at the dig, *not* to go off by yourselves.'

'Before you say any more, listen to *me*!' Frankie said in a rude voice. 'This is our half-term holiday. We aren't at school now. And we aren't your servants!'

Regan grabbed Frankie's arm.

'Hey, calm down, Frankie,' she said. 'Mrs Tinker was worried about us. You mustn't be rude.'

'Leave me alone!' Frankie shouted. 'All of you – leave me alone! I'm going to my tent!'

———

Two hours later, Frankie came out of her tent. She apologised to Mrs Tinker. By supper-time, everyone was friends again.

After the meal, Leo showed the kids some things which had been found at the dig. There were lots of animal bones and some broken pots.

'Did you find many coins on the site?' Jack asked.

'No, we didn't find any,' Leo answered.

'Frankie found a coin – or she found half of one,' Mrs Tinker said. 'I'll show it to you, Leo.'

'I've got a better idea,' Leo said. 'We're going to have a visitor here tomorrow. His name is Edward Musgrave. He knows all about coins. You must show the coin to him. And he will probably tell you more about Eleanor's story too.'

7

The Lovers

Edward Musgrave arrived at the dig at about lunchtime the next day. Mr Musgrave was a strange old man. His hair was long and white. His face was white too. He was wearing black clothes, a big hat and a black tie.

'Tell us about Eleanor. What do you know about her?' Regan asked him. 'Did she throw herself off that bridge or didn't she?'

'I've never believed that part of the story,' Mr Musgrave said. 'But I'll tell you Eleanor's story from the beginning. And this is the *real* story. It's not the story which was told by the Glanville family.'

'First of all, you must understand something. Eleanor hated Hugo Glanville,' Mr Musgrave said. 'She was his ward, but she did not like his treatment of her. And most of all she hated the idea of marriage to his neighbour. She did not want to marry an old man because she was in love with a young man. He was a young man from the village, and his name was Todd Blakely. Hugo knew this. So he tried to get Todd out of the way.'

'How did he do that?' Frankie asked. 'Did Hugo kill Todd?'

'No, Todd killed Hugo,' the old man replied. 'But that was probably a mistake. It happened at Isenglas Hall. One day, Todd stole a rabbit from the park. He probably wanted food for his family. Hugo found out about this and tried to catch the young man. The squire wanted to punish him. But Todd ran away. So Hugo spoke to Eleanor again about marrying the rich old neighbour.'

'This neighbour wanted Hugo's land,' Mr Musgrave continued. 'Eleanor was going to own the squire's land when he died. That was why the neighbour was going to marry Eleanor. It was Hugo's land that he wanted, not Eleanor. He didn't love her at all.'

'How terrible!' Tom said. 'What happened next?'

'Todd went to Isenglas Hall one night,' Mr Musgrave replied. 'I don't know *why* he went. Maybe he wanted to talk to Hugo. Maybe he'd decided to take Eleanor away. But there was a fight and Hugo was killed. He was stabbed with Todd's knife.'

'It was an accident!' Frankie said quickly. 'It *wasn't* murder – it was an accident.'

'Yes, I think that too,' Mr Musgrave said. 'But Hugo's servants heard the noise of the fight. Todd left the house quickly, but the servants ran after him.'

'What about Eleanor?' Regan asked. 'Did she leave the Hall with Todd?'

'Nobody is sure about that,' the old man replied. 'But Eleanor was never seen again after that night.'

'*Did* she drown herself?' Tom asked.

'Hugo's neighbour wanted Isenglas Hall and all the squire's land,' Mr Musgrave said. '*He* said that Eleanor was dead. The servants told everyone the same story. So Hugo's neighbour took everything. He didn't look for Eleanor. He had Hugo's land and he was happy.

'The servants caught Todd,' Edward Musgrave went on. 'He was hiding in the graveyard – in the Glanville family vault.'

'And they hanged him – is that right?' Jack said.

'Yes, that's right,' Mr Musgrave replied. 'Hugo's servants hanged Todd from a tree in the graveyard.'

'Hugo's servants hanged Todd from a tree in the graveyard.'

'How sad they were – Todd and Eleanor,' Frankie said quietly.

'What *did* happen to Eleanor?' Regan asked the old man. 'What do *you* think? Did she get away? She didn't drown herself, did she?'

'No one knows the answer to that,' Mr Musgrave said.

The kids said nothing. They were thinking about the graveyard and the vault. All that horror! All that fear! Those feelings had lasted for over two hundred years. What a sad story! The kids were very quiet.

———

A few minutes later, Mrs Tinker came out of her tent.

'I can't find it!' she said. 'Frankie gave me that half-coin. I was taking care of it. Now it's gone. I'm sorry, Frankie.'

Then Mrs Tinker looked around.

'Where *is* Frankie?' she said.

'I don't know,' Jack said. 'She was here a minute ago. Maybe Mr Musgrave's story upset her. She'll be back soon.'

But Frankie did not come back. After lunch, Leo and Mr Musgrave went into the town. The other three kids worked hard at the dig with their teacher. But Mrs Tinker was getting more and more worried about Frankie.

'Shall we search for her?' Regan said.

Mrs Tinker thought for a few moments before she replied.

'No, not yet,' she said. 'Frankie is upset. She wants to be alone. She'll be back soon – I'm sure of that.'

But the children were unhappy about their friend. Frankie had changed. Something evil was changing her!

———

The mist came back again later in the afternoon. The mist came from the graveyard and it covered the park around Isenglas Hall. It came nearer and nearer to the site of the dig.

'Where *has* Frankie gone?' Mrs Tinker said to the kids. 'I'm very worried about her now. Do you know anything, Regan. What did Frankie say to you?'

'Nothing,' Regan replied quickly. 'Maybe she went into the town. Yes, that's what she did. Look for her there, Mrs Tinker.'

Mrs Tinker thought about what Regan had said.

'I'll do that,' she said at last. 'But you must all stay here. Do you understand? Stay here, on the site.'

'OK. We'll wait here for Frankie,' Regan said. 'She'll soon be back. I know that.'

Mrs Tinker nodded. She got into her car and drove quickly away towards the town.

'Now we'll look for Frankie ourselves,' Regan said. 'She's *not* in the town. She's somewhere near here. Come on, we must find her. I'll go down to the lake. Jack, you go to the little bridge.'

'And I'll go back to the graveyard,' Tom said.

8

Frankie's New Friend

Tom was standing alone by the graveyard gate. The thick mist was all around him. The boy felt very afraid. He did not want to walk into that terrible graveyard! He moved forward slowly.

Suddenly, Tom heard a harsh cry overhead. A big black bird was flying towards the church. Then Tom saw the old tree. Its black branches stretched out towards him.

Frankie was standing under the tree. She did not move.

'Frankie! What are you doing here?' Tom said. 'Hey, listen to me, Frankie. What's wrong?'

Frankie did not answer Tom's questions. She did not speak to him at all. Tears were running down her face.

'They hanged Todd from this terrible tree,' she said.

'That happened a long time ago,' Tom said. 'Come back with me now, please, Frankie. We're all very worried about you.'

Frankie did not answer. She turned and ran out of the graveyard. She ran quickly into the white mist.

Tom did not know what to do. Why was Frankie behaving so strangely?

———

Regan was walking by the lake. Again and again she called Frankie's name. But there was no answer. The American girl walked on until she was near the little building by the end of the lake.

Then Regan heard a voice. It was Frankie's voice! Frankie was talking to someone.

'Hey! Frankie!' Regan called, as she ran to her friend. 'What are you doing here?'

In a moment, Regan was standing beside the older girl.

'Who were you talking to?' she asked her. 'There's no one here.'

'I was talking to a boy,' Frankie replied. 'He's a friend – a new friend. You mustn't tell anyone about him. Do you understand, Regan?'

'Oh, yes. I understand,' Regan said. 'You've got a boyfriend. But where did you meet this boy?'

'I met him here,' Frankie replied. 'Let's go back to the others now. I don't want Mrs Tinker to worry about me.'

'She's worried about you already!' Regan said. 'You left the camp hours ago.'

Suddenly, Frankie looked at her watch.

'Is that the time?' she said in surprise.

———

'I'm sorry,' Frankie told Mrs Tinker. 'I had a headache. I wanted to be alone.'

It was an hour after Regan had found Frankie by the lake. Mrs Tinker had returned to the camp.

'I was very worried about you,' Mrs Tinker said. 'I have to take care of all of you. Please don't go away by yourself, Frankie.'

'I promise,' Frankie said.

'Good! Then you must all promise the same thing,' the teacher said. 'No one must go off alone.'

Regan did not tell the others about Frankie's 'new friend'. And Tom said nothing about his meeting with Frankie in the graveyard. But both of them were very worried about her.

———

That night, everyone had supper with Leo. Leo's caravan was near the site and it was large and comfortable. Outside its windows, the mist was very thick.

'Is someone out there calling me?' Frankie asked herself.

'Let's play a game,' Leo said. 'It's the game called "Murder in the Dark". Do you know it?'

'I don't,' Frankie said. 'Tell us about it, Leo.'

'First, everyone must be blindfolded,' Leo said. 'Everyone except me.'

He picked up some narrow strips of black cloth.

'I'll tie one of these strips over everyone's eyes,' Leo said. 'Then you won't be able to see anyone – you'll be blindfolded. After that, I'm going to tell you a story. I have a few objects that you must feel while I'm telling the story. You'll be able to feel them, but you won't be able to *see* them.'

When everyone was blindfolded, Leo began his story.

'It was a dark night,' Leo said. 'The mist was very thick outside the windows. Five friends were sitting in the dark. They heard a noise outside. They heard footsteps. The footsteps were loud and heavy – bang, bang, bang. Then something pushed the door open – BANG! What was it? It was a terrible monster! The huge monster was carrying a bag and a knife. And the knife was covered in *blood*!

' "I am a murderer," the monster said. "I killed a man and I cut up his body. The pieces of his body are in my bag – hair, eyes, brains. I want you to feel them. Hold out your hands!" '

Leo put something into Mrs Tinker's hands.

'Oh! It's horrible!' she said. Then she passed it on to Regan. Leo continued his story.

' "That's the man's hair. It's covered in blood," the monster said. "And this is one of his eyes!" '

The 'horrible things' were passed from one person to another. The hair was really some pieces of string covered with jam. And the eye was a grape.

Leo put a grape into Frankie's hand. She felt the soft round fruit and she started to laugh. But suddenly, the thing in her hand had a horrible smell. Frankie felt very sick. She pulled the piece of cloth away from her eyes. Then she looked at her hands.

Frankie's hands were covered with blood! The blood was dripping onto her jeans. And there was a blood-covered eye in her hand!

Frankie screamed and jumped up. Then someone was holding her. She turned and turned but she could not escape. Everything was red! She was in a red mist! She closed her eyes and she screamed again.

'Frankie, be quiet! It's OK,' Mrs Tinker was saying.

Frankie opened her eyes. She looked down at her hands. There was no blood, and there was no eye. There was only a grape. She looked at her friends' worried faces.

'I'm sorry,' Frankie said. 'I saw — but everything is OK now.'

Jack was watching Frankie carefully. Something bad had happened to her. And it wasn't finished yet – Jack was sure of that. He was very afraid.

———

In the middle of the night, Frankie woke up. The boy was there again. She spoke to him quietly.

'Was it your blood?' she asked. 'I was very afraid.'

'Don't be afraid. I'm fine,' the boy said. 'And don't worry – I'm not going away. We can help each other.'

'We can help each other,' Frankie repeated. 'I understand. I'm safe now. But you are so lonely.'

Frankie was holding the half-coin in her hand. She closed her eyes. Tears ran down her face. The boy was sad and lonely. She had to help him!

9

'I Must Find Eleanor'

Regan slept badly that night. She had lots of strange dreams and she woke up very early. It was only six o'clock! Regan looked over at Frankie's sleeping bag. It was empty.

'There's something wrong with that girl,' Regan said to herself. She got up and looked out of the tent. Frankie was walking quickly away from the campsite. She was walking towards Isenglas Hall.

Regan dressed quickly. She ran to the boys' tent.

'Wake up!' she called. 'Get dressed! We must follow Frankie. Hurry!'

The three friends were soon following Frankie across the park. They could see her footprints in the wet grass.

'There's something wrong with Frankie,' Regan said.

'We know. We're not stupid,' Tom said.

Frankie's footprints were leading them to the Hall. Soon they saw the old building. It looked frightening.

The Hall was a ruin. It had broken walls and broken windows. Grass and plants were growing over it. There were pieces of wood fixed over the lower windows.

The three friends walked towards the porch of the house. The porch had thin stone pillars. There was a triangle of stone on top, joining the tops of the pillars. Inside the porch was the main door of the Hall. The door had pieces of wood fixed over it. Frankie was there. She was pulling at the wood with her hands.

'I want to get this wood off the door,' Frankie said. ' I must get inside the Hall. Help me, you three.'

At that moment, the piece of wood which she was pulling broke. Frankie fell back against one of the pillars. There was a loud noise. The pillar broke and the heavy stone roof of the porch began to fall. Jack ran towards Frankie and pushed her out of the way. As she fell to the ground, the stone roof fell too. The roof hit the ground one metre from the girl.

Frankie took no notice of the accident. She got up and pulled at the wood again. Jack could not believe it. He pushed her away from the door.

Frankie said nothing, but she hit Jack hard. This time, both of them fell on the ground. Frankie stared at her friend angrily.

'Why are you here?' she asked. 'Why did you follow me? Leave me alone!'

Frankie stood up. Then she saw something in Jack's hand. It was the half-coin.

'Give me that!' she screamed. 'It's mine! It fell out of my pocket. Give it to me now!'

Jack held out the half-coin and Frankie grabbed it.

'You're all horrible,' she said. 'I don't want your help.'

'What *do* you want, Frankie?' Jack said kindly.

'I want to find Eleanor,' she said. 'And you three are stopping me.'

Frankie looked at the half-coin. Then she put it in her pocket. Without a word, she began to walk back towards the campsite.

Regan, Jack and Tom looked at each other.

'There's something terrible inside Frankie,' Jack said. 'There's something in her mind. And it's very strong. It will hurt Frankie if we don't stop it. And there's something bad around here. It's here at the Hall and it's in the vault. It's by the river too.'

'I saw Frankie crying under a tree yesterday,' Tom said.

'And I heard her talking to a boy yesterday,' Regan said. 'But I couldn't see him. Was he a ghost?'

'There aren't any ghosts,' Tom said.

'I'm not sure about that,' Jack said. 'But Frankie is in danger. I *am* sure of that. We must all help her.'

'Don't worry, I'll talk to her,' Regan said. 'We'll be here for two more days. I'll find out the truth!'

10

Todd Blakely

Back at the campsite, Frankie was cooking breakfast. She was smiling happily.

'There's no work this morning,' Mrs Tinker said. 'We'll all go into the town. You can do some shopping and buy postcards. And we'll have lunch there too.'

Everyone enjoyed the morning. After a good lunch, they started their journey back to the campsite.

———

The mist had returned, and it was thicker than before. Mrs Tinker drove very slowly and carefully.

When they got back to the dig, they all went into Leo's caravan. It was warm there. The children played games and wrote postcards. Later, Mrs Tinker went to her tent to read. Suddenly, Frankie stood up.

'I'm going out for a walk,' she said.

Her friends looked at each other. Frankie saw this.

'I'm not going far,' Frankie said. 'I'll be OK!'

She shut the door with a bang.

'I'll follow her,' Jack said to the others. 'She won't see me in this mist.'

———

Frankie walked quickly away from the campsite. She walked past the site of the village and on towards the lake.

The boy was waiting for her in the little stone building at the end of the lake. He was sitting on the stone seat. His black hair hung down over his face. He looked very ill and unhappy.

'Did you get it?' he asked Frankie. His voice was deep.

'No, the others stopped me,' she replied. 'I didn't get into the house.'

'You *must* get it!' the boy said wildly.

'Yes, I know that,' Frankie said. 'I'm sorry.'

'Go to the house again,' the boy said coldly.

A few metres away, Jack was hiding behind a pillar. He could hear Frankie's voice. She was talking to someone, but no one was answering her. Who was she talking to? There was no one there.

Frankie spoke to the boy again.

'Tell me something,' she said. 'You killed Hugo Glanville that night in the Hall. It was an accident, wasn't it?'

The boy put his hands over his face. He spoke very quietly now. 'I went there to see Eleanor,' he said. 'The squire caught me. He hit me and I took out my knife. He ran towards me and he fell onto the knife. I pushed him away. But my knife was in his chest. There was blood everywhere.'

The boy was shaking now. Frankie put her hand on his arm. He looked at her.

'The servants heard the noise,' he continued. 'They saw me, but I jumped from the window. I ran and ran.'

'You ran to the vault,' Frankie said. 'You tried to hide there.'

'Yes, that's right. But the servants found me. They pulled me out and —'

The boy stopped speaking.

'I know what happened,' Frankie said. 'They hanged you from that tree in the graveyard.'

'What happened to Eleanor?' the boy said.

'No one knows,' Frankie replied.

'She had the other half of the coin,' he said. He looked at Frankie with his sad, dark eyes.

'You found my half of the coin,' he went on. 'You took me out of the darkness. Now you must find Eleanor's half. Then she will wake too.'

The boy stood up. He held Frankie's arm with his thin fingers.

'The other half of the coin is in Isenglas Hall. I'm sure of that,' he said. 'Find it and bring it to me.'

'Come and help me,' Frankie said.

'No, I can't go into the Hall,' the boy replied sadly. 'I can't go there because the squire's blood stops me. You must go alone this time. Don't tell your friends.'

'That will be difficult,' Frankie said. 'They'll try to follow me.'

Suddenly there was a noise nearby. The boy looked up. His face was very angry.

'There's someone there,' he said. 'Someone followed you here!'

Frankie turned.

'I can't see anyone,' she said. She turned back again, but the boy was not there.

'Todd! Todd! Come back!' she shouted.

At that moment, Jack came out from behind a pillar.

'You fool!' Frankie said. 'What are you doing here? He's gone! He's gone! And it's your fault, Jack!' She shouted again, 'Come back, Todd!'

'Frankie, tell me. Who was here?' Jack asked.

'Todd, of course. Todd Blakely. You saw him yourself.'

'No, Frankie. I didn't see him,' Jack replied gently. 'There was no one here. You were talking to yourself.'

Frankie laughed angrily.

'You're never wrong, are you, Jack?' she said. 'But you are wrong this time. Todd wants *me* to help him, not you. This time, you can't help me or Todd.'

'But Todd is dead!' Jack shouted. 'The servants hanged Todd Blakely two hundred years ago!'

Frankie did not answer. She pushed past Jack and ran into the mist. This time, Jack did not follow her.

———

Frankie was under the tree in the graveyard now. A black shape hung from the tree. It was the body of Todd Blakely. His black eyes were open but there was no life in them. Frankie touched his hand. It was cold.

'I've got your half-coin. But I'm afraid they'll take it from me again. Do you want it now?' Frankie said.

A big black bird flew overhead. It landed in the tree and it gave a loud, sad cry. It was an answer to the girl's question.

'Yes, I understand,' Frankie said. She knelt down under the tree. She dug in the ground with her fingers. Then she dropped the half-coin into the little hole. She covered it with some earth.

'It will be safe there,' Frankie said. 'I'll come back soon.'

The black bird cried again. A black shape flew from the tree. It flew away into the mist. Frankie walked slowly back to the camp.

11

Isenglas Hall

Regan was waiting for Frankie at the campsite. At last she saw her friend coming.

'Hey, Frankie! Where have you been?' Regan asked with a smile.

'I've been walking,' Frankie said. 'Is there a problem?'

'No, no,' Regan said. 'Do you want a hot drink?'

'No, thank you,' Frankie replied. 'I'm tired. I'm going to our tent. And I don't want any supper this evening. I'm not hungry.'

———

At nine o'clock that night, Regan went into her tent. She shone her torch on Frankie's sleeping bag.

'Hey, Frankie. I want to talk to you,' she said.

Frankie opened her eyes. She shook her head.

'Not now. Not in the dark,' she said. 'I'll talk to you in the morning. OK?'

'OK,' Regan said. 'Sleep well!'

Regan had bad dreams again that night. In one dream, she saw the head of a dead person in her sleeping bag. Its rotting teeth smiled at her. She woke up shaking with fear. It was the middle of the night, but she was afraid to sleep again.

She pushed at Frankie's sleeping bag.

'Wake up, Frankie! Wake up!' Regan said.

She pushed at the bag again. It was empty. Frankie was not there.

'I can't look for her by myself. I'm too afraid,' Regan said. 'I must wake the boys.'

Soon the three friends were dressed and standing outside their tents. The night air was cold. The moon was big and very bright. Everything looked black and white in the moonlight.

'Something bad is going to happen tonight,' Jack said. 'But where? Must we go to the Hall or to the river?'

'We must go to the Hall,' Regan said. 'Frankie is there, I'm sure of that.'

'Yes, you're right,' Jack said. 'Come on, let's go quickly. We must help Frankie. She's our friend and she's in trouble.'

Regan and the boys walked quickly towards the old, ruined Hall. Jack was feeling very worried. There was something evil there – something very old and very evil.

The ruined house was waiting for them! The porch was dark and misty, and the big wooden door was open. Fear came out from the darkness of the house.

The kids switched on their torches. Jack led the way into the house. Tom was the last to enter. He heard a noise and he looked up at the sky. A big black bird flew across the moon. Tom was very afraid, but he followed the others into the house.

Soon the three friends were in a dark passage. By the light of their torches, they saw a wooden picture of the wolf and the child. The same picture was carved in the stone of the Glanville family vault.

There were doors at both ends of the passage.

'I'll go this way, to the right,' Jack said.

'I'll come with you,' Regan said.

'I'll go the other way,' Tom said. He turned to the left. He shone his torch in front of him.

The kids reached the doors at the same moment. Then their torches went out. There was no light at all. Suddenly, a wind rushed along the passage, up and down, round and round. There was a horrible smell in the passage. It was an old, evil smell – the smell of something very bad.

'Be careful,' Jack called to his brother.

'Yes, I'll be careful!' Tom answered. He pushed open the door in front of him. He entered a room.

Moonlight shone through some high windows. The light shone on chairs and tables. It shone on paintings and on silver dishes.

There were some stairs, leading up to another floor. A young woman was standing on the stairs. She had golden hair. She was wearing a long, white dress.

Tom closed his eyes and then he looked again. No, it wasn't a woman. It was a girl – a girl dressed in a T-shirt and jeans. It was Frankie!

'Frankie!' Tom shouted. He moved forward.

But suddenly, he was alone. The stairs were broken and the room was empty and ruined. There were no chairs or tables. There were no paintings or silver dishes.

Where was Frankie?

12

The Secret Room

'Frankie!'

Jack and Regan heard Tom shouting. They turned and they ran along the passage and through the door. Tom was standing in the middle of the big, ruined room.

'Frankie was here,' Tom said. His body was shaking. 'I saw her. She was climbing the stairs.'

'No one could climb those stairs – not even a ghost,' Regan said.

'But Frankie *did* go upstairs,' Tom told her. 'I *saw* her. Let's find some other stairs and look for her on the upper floor.'

The three kids went back to the other end of the passage. They walked slowly through dark, empty rooms. The friends were all very, very frightened. They saw evil things standing in the shadows. The house seemed full of ghosts. They followed the kids through the terrible, empty rooms.

'Stop it!' Regan shouted to the ghosts. 'You can't frighten us! We're going to find Frankie! Go away!'

For a few minutes, the ghosts *did* go away. Then they came back. And now a terrible feeling of fear came with them!

The kids found some stairs which were not broken. They ran up the stairs to the upper floor. There was fear here too and also a deep, deep sadness.

'What terrible thing happened here?' Regan asked herself.

They walked through a door into a narrow room.

There was a window at the end of the room. Frankie was sitting near it. She did not move.

Regan started to walk towards her friend. But Jack stopped her.

Regan looked down. There was no floor between them and the window.

Frankie stood up. She walked towards them.

'Be careful, Frankie! You'll fall!' Regan shouted.

But Frankie did *not* fall. She walked across the empty space, towards the door! Then she walked past her friends without speaking.

Regan ran after her and grabbed the girl's arm.

'It's me, Frankie!' Regan shouted. 'Where are you going? Stay with us, Frankie! *Please* stay with us!'

Frankie pushed Regan hard, but Regan held onto her arm. Frankie screamed and screamed. She fought her friend. She wanted to get away. The boys ran up to help Regan, but they were too late. Suddenly, Frankie was free and she was running.

———

Frankie was very afraid. 'I must get away from this house,' she told herself. 'Something evil is following me. It must not catch me!'

Frankie ran quickly through room after room. In her mind, the rooms were clean and full of beautiful things. Paintings hung on the walls. And there were tapestries – pictures made from cloth and coloured wool. The colours were clear and bright.

Frankie stopped in front of one of the large beautiful tapestries. Something very bad was behind it – she knew that. But she had to find out what it was.

Frankie pulled at the heavy tapestry. It fell from the

wall onto the floor. She pushed at the wooden wall with her fingers. A piece of wood moved. She pushed the wall again and a little door opened. It was a door into a secret room.

Moonlight was shining into the room. There was a terrible smell in there. It was the smell of death!

A large chest stood in the centre of the room. The big wooden box looked very old. The chest had a lock with a big black key in it.

'I must open this chest,' Frankie said to herself.

The girl turned the key. She opened the heavy wooden lid. She looked down into the chest. Horror and fear filled her mind. Everything went black. The darkness covered her. She screamed and fell down into the darkness.

———

'She's gone! Frankie's gone!' Regan was shouting in the long, narrow room. 'Which way did she go? We must follow her. Listen!'

Tom, Jack and Regan stood still. They did not speak. But the old house was full of strange noises. They heard footsteps everywhere.

'This way,' Regan said. She ran through the empty rooms and the boys ran after her.

They came to the room with the tapestries. But the tapestries they saw were old and dusty. Regan was the first to enter the secret room. The black chest was open. Frankie was lying on the floor beside it. Her eyes were closed.

'It's OK, she's alive,' Regan said. She knelt beside her friend and held her hand. Frankie's eyes opened.

The chest seemed full of a deep, black sadness. Tom walked towards it.

*The black chest was open. Frankie was lying on the floor
beside it.*

'No! Don't look in there!' Jack shouted.

There was something in the chest. No – it was some-one, not something! Tom saw bones covered with thin, dried skin. And he saw a head which had terrible smiling teeth. There was some golden hair too and pieces of a white dress. And there was a half-coin in the dead girl's boney hand.

'It's Eleanor,' Frankie said. She was sitting up now. Her face was pale and her eyes were sad.

'How did she get in there?' Regan asked.

'Hugo put her there,' Frankie said. 'Eleanor did not want to marry the old neighbour. So Hugo locked her in the chest, to punish her. He often did that. Usually, he kept her there for a few hours. Then he let her out.

'But the last time, Hugo could not let Eleanor out,' Frankie went on. 'Hugo was dead. He had been killed by Todd's knife. No one knew where Eleanor was. So she died in the chest.'

Frankie stood up. She looked down at Eleanor's bones. She took the half-coin from the dead girl's hand. She held it in front of her.

'It's all right now, Todd,' she said in a loud voice. 'I'll join the two halves together. Then you can both rest in peace.'

———

Frankie led the way out of the ruins of Isenglas Hall. The night air was very cold. The kids walked through the park in silence. They walked to the tree in the graveyard.

Frankie knelt down. She dug the other half-coin from the ground.

'The squire's servants hanged Todd here,' she said. 'I can't join the half-coins together in this sad place. Come on, we'll go to the deserted village.'

The moon had disappeared now. The night was very dark in the half hour before sunrise.

Soon, the four friends stood together by the site of the village. Frankie held out her arms. Then she brought the two pieces of the old coin together.

As she stood there, Frankie saw the village as it had been long before. The houses were all complete. Light came from some of the windows. A few happy people were walking in the narrow streets. Todd and Eleanor stood there too, hand in hand. They looked at Frankie and smiled.

Frankie was smiling too.

Then the village disappeared and suddenly it was morning. Frankie cried out and pointed to the sky. Two black birds were flying away, into the morning light. All the kids saw them.

Frankie's face was wet with tears. But she was laughing too.

'It's OK now,' she said. 'Eleanor and Todd are together at last. We can all rest now.'

'Let's all go back to bed for a few hours,' Regan said.

Frankie laughed again. 'A few hours?' she said. 'I could sleep for a week!'

The four friends walked back to their tents. The long, dark night was over.

————

Later that morning, a part of Isenglas Hall fell down. Workmen came to make the ruins safe. They found Eleanor's body in the old chest. A few days later, the body was buried in the old graveyard. The evil had gone and the two lovers were at peace at last.

Points for Understanding

1

'You British people use some strange phrases,' Regan says. But Tom, Jack and Frankie don't understand the words on the plaque either. Why? Make a guess.

2

At first, Frankie cannot climb out of the vault. Why not?

3

Why did Hugo Glanville destroy the village?

4

Frankie sees a young man standing in the shadows. Who is he? Make a guess.

5

'Frankie is doing some strange things,' says Jack. What does he mean?

6

Jack hears a deep voice in the Glanville family vault. Whose voice is it? Make a guess.

7

Mr Musgrave tells the kids about Hugo's death. 'It was an accident,' Frankie says. Why does she say this? Make a guess.

8

What does 'blindfolded' mean?

9

After his fight with Frankie, Jack has Frankie's half-coin. How did he get it? Make a guess.

10

Frankie sees a big black bird in the graveyard. The children often see this bird. Why does it appear at this point in the story? Make a guess.

11

In the Hall, Tom sees some paintings and some silver dishes. Then they disappear. What is happening? Make a guess.

12

'Eleanor and Todd are together at last,' Frankie says. Why does she say this?

Published by Macmillan Heinemann ELT
Between Towns Road, Oxford OX4 3PP
Macmillan Heinemann ELT is an imprint of
Macmillan Publishers Limited
Companies and representatives throughout the world
Heinemann is a registered trademark of Harcourt Education, used under licence.

ISBN 978 0 2300 3699 4
ISBN 978 1 4050 7666 1 (with CD pack)

Unquiet Graves © Allan Frewin Jones 1999
First published in Great Britain by Macmillan Children's Books 1999

This retold version by Margaret Tarner for Macmillan Readers
First published 2002
Text © Macmillan Publishers Limited 2002, 2005
Design and illustration © Macmillan Publishers Limited 2002, 2005

This edition first published 2005

Designed by Sue Vaudin
Illustrated by Annabel Large
Original cover template design by Jackie Hill
Cover illustration by Liz Cooke

Printed in Thailand
2010 2009 2008
5 4 3 2 1

with CD pack
2009 2008 2007
7 6 5 4 3